It Will Happen In February!

by
Michael X

SAUCERIAN PUBLISHER

ISBN: 9781955087001

© 2022, Saucerian Publisher

TABLE OF CONTENTS

INTRODUCTION

It is generally a good idea to return to the classics in any genre. This also goes for UFO literature. Rereading a book, or reviewing old documents after ten or twenty years is a rewarding experience. You will discover new data and ideas you didn´t notice before. The reason, of course, is that you are, in many ways, not the same person reading the book the second or third time. Hopefully you have advanced in knowledge, experience, intellectual and spiritual discernment. A good starting point is to reread the contactee classics material of the 1950s, in order to understand the deeper mystery involved in what happened during that era.

Contactee is the name that has been given to people, especially since the 1950s, who claim contact with extraterrestrials, beings from other planets. In the wake of the citing of flying saucers by pilot Kenneth Arnold in 1947, speculation was rampant that they were possibly spaceships from a distant planet . This group included George Adamski (1891–1965), the pioneer, and his quickly emerging competitors: Truman Bethurum (1898–1969), George Van Tassel (1910–1978), Daniel W. Fry (1908–1992), Orfeo Angelucci (1912–1993), George King (1919–1997), Buck Nelson (1894–1982), and about as many others, more obscure. The era came to an abrupt end in the US with Betty Hill (1920–2004), who introduced a new paradigm to replace Adamski's stereotypical Space Brothers.

Following the Adamski tradition, one of the most influential contactees of that era was a man named Michael Barton, who wrote several books under the pen name of Michael X. Michael Dimond Barton was born on May 26, 1937 in Seatle, Washington, and died on June 26, 2003 in Los Angeles, California. He was the son of Claude Coffee Barton, and Elva Lois Dimond. He had a brother: Jerry Keith Barton. He died on June26, 2003 in Los Angeles, California. There is not much information about Michael X Barton available. Michael Barton was one of the most influential contactees of that 50's & 60's who wrote several books under the pen name of Michael X. Michael Dimond Barton was born on May 26, 1937 in Seatle, Washington, and died on June 26, 2003 in Los Angeles, California. He was the son of Claude Coffee Barton, and Elva Lois Dimond. He had a brother: Jerry Keith Barton. He died on June26, 2003 in Los Angeles, California. There is not much information about Michael X Barton available. Here is a brief biographical note taken from the edition of *Secrets of Higher Contact:* "Michael X. Barton is widely know for his New-Age writings, and has been a prolific author in the Metaphysical and Inspirational field since 1949. Thousands of persons from all walks of life,who are seeking higher Truth and Wisdom, find a wealth of New-Age Information and guidance in his easy -to-read writings. In 1940, Michael's own inner development was

Barton-Scott wedding

Michael Dimond Barton (right) and Jerry Keith Barton (left)

Michael Dimond Barton

In FamilySearch Family Tree

Save this record and choose the information you want to add to your family tree

Name	Michael Dimond Barton
Gender	Male
Birth	May 26 1937 ⚲ Seattle, King, Washington, United States
Death	June 26 2003 ⚲ Newhall, Los Angeles, California, United States
Burial	July 19 2003 ⚲ Federal Way, King, Washington, United States
Parents	Claude Coffey Barton Elva Lois Barton (born Dimond)
Son	Marc Dimond Barton
Brother	Jerry Keith Barton
Source	Click here to view record on FamilySearch

Barton's Family Tree. Taken from MyHeritage

Man From Venus To Lecture Here
Santa Cruz Sentinel (Santa Cruz, California)
05 Nov 1959, Thu.Page 7

accelerated in a dramatic and, positive way, when he was contacted briefly by a white-garbed Master from the higher planes of life. Michael's inner eye was opened temporarily and he could see the Being clearly. From this time on, Michael pursue the Higher Truth. He organized and taught a "Self-Unfoldment" class in 1960, with great success. In 1961, Michael X, Barton received the honorary degree of Doctor of Divinity from Dr. John W. Hopkins, president of Williams College in Berkeley, California, Michael is also a fully ordained minister of the Universal Life Church of Modesto, California. "Michael" is alse known for his interesting and informative lectures on New-Age topics, He has spoken to attentive audiences in many cities in California, Arizona and Nevada since 1954. A fascinating column, entitled, "A Look in The Crystal", which appears as a regular feature in the *Cosmic Star* newspaper, is written by Michael. In 1964, a "Cosmic Visitor" apparently from a much higher dimension than our own limited three-dimensional world, cortacted Michael. The contact was made by a vision, in full color, in which the "Visitor" revealed his presence to Michel. This Cosmic Being gives no name, but states tha: he is "the Truth, the Light, and the ALL in the Universe." The Visitor is entirely REAL. He is responsible for an amazing phenomenon (a picture of an Angel in an old print called The First Christmas Morn, has been weeping real tears frequent intervals since 1961), and other supernormal manifestations. The Cosmic Visitor has made a tremendous PREDICTION. It concerns an impending COSMIC event that will be world-transforming! Michael X. Barton's thrilling book entitled, "The Weeping Angel Prediction", tells the full story of the Cosmic Visitor and his prophecy, and documents many of the incredible manifestations now occurring all over the world. Michael X Barton is not a spokesman for any earthly Church system of religion, "My ministry," he says, "is Universal Trulh and Higher Evolution".

iv

The first time Michael X appeared in the American newspaper was on Nov 5, 1959, on page 7 of the Santa Cruz Sentinel. He gave a lecture entitled: *The Great Venusian Message* to promote his booklet *Venusian's Secret Science* to the members of the Santa Cruz Understanding Unit 9. It is essential to point out that Barton was a self-proclaimed "NewAge Seer".

During the early '60s, Barton started a series of talks on UFOs around Northern and Southern California. He gave lectures with other contactees like Frank E Stranges, and Daniel Fry's Understanding Units. Also, at this time, he was a minister, like Stranges, and it seems that he was affiliated to the Stranges' Church: The International Evangelism Crusades Inc.In addition, he gave lectures at the *Aquarian Cosmic Color Fellowship* in Los Angeles. During this time, the main topics of Barton's lectures were about: "Flying saucer Sightings," "Astral Projections," "The Coming World Peril," and "The Seven Rays of Healing", "World UFO Predictions and You".

Frank E Stranges. Photo taken from the opening satement of " The Dalotek Affair". This was the seventeenth episode aired of the first series of UFO- a 1970 British television science fiction series about an alien invasion of Earth. The episode was filmed between 15 July to 25 July 1969 and aired on the ATV Midlands on 10 February 1971. Stranges was interviewed by australian actor Keith Alexander.

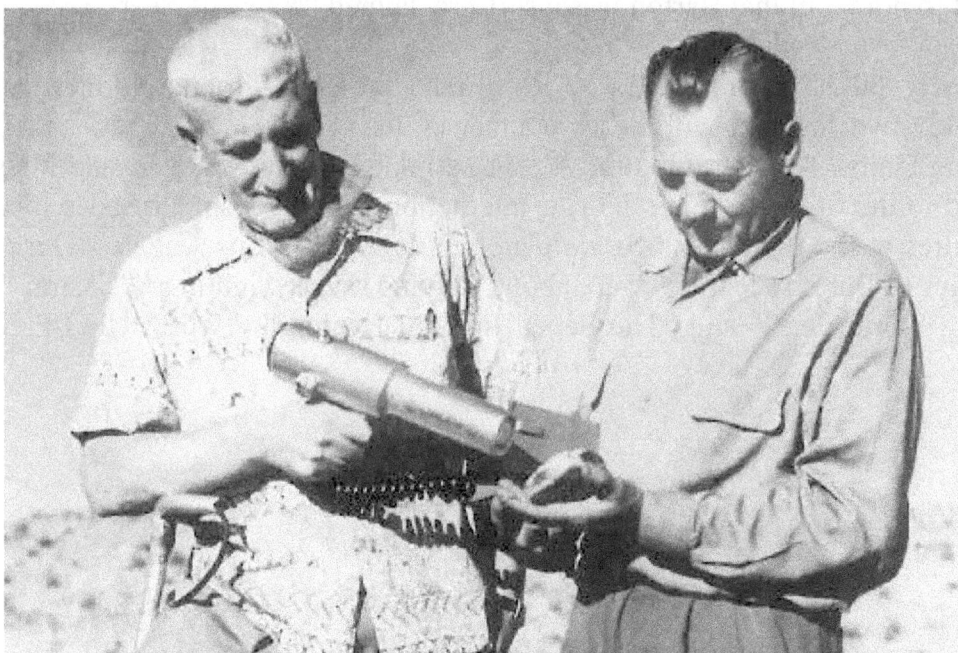

Frank Scully and Daniel Fry in the May June 1995 issue of International UFO Reporter.

There is a lecturer by the name of Violet Ballard Barton that gave a talk on the topic of "Mark Twain as a Mystic Helper" at a New Age conference held at Harmony Grove on January 5 & 6, 1963. Barton was the main speaker of this meeting with a lecture entitled: "For Ever Young." We do not know if Violet is a relative of Michael Barton.

According to the newspaper's review for this short biography on Barton, it seems that Barton rarely gave lectures to outside groups from Fry's California Understanding local chapters. The last known public showing of Barton, according to these clips, was in November 1966 at the Universal Life Church in Modesto, California. He talked about life after death and life on other planets at this meeting. We could not find any more news articles under Michael X. However; there is no doubt that Barton continues lecturing after this date.

During his life, Barton was influenced by other contactees like: George Adamski, George Van Tassel, Dan Fry, and Orfeo Angelucci, according to his statement in his Flying Saucer Revelations but especially Van Tassel. Barton attended Van Tassel's second Giant Rock Interplanetary Spacecraft Convention at Landers Field, held on Saturday, 12 March 1955. At this meeting, Barton was inspired to put together an educational and inspirational course of study dealing with interplanetary subjects entitled: Flying Saucer Revelations. The influence of VanTassel on Barton is undeniable as he describes with wonder Van Tassel's experience:

*On August 2t4h of 1953, George Van Tassel of Giant Rock in
Yucca Valley, California, was wakened out of his sleep around 2 A. M..
The strange Jvitor who stood before him at the foot of his bed
spoke to him, saying: "My name is Solgonda, I would be pleased to
show you our craft."Pp.12.*

George Van Tassel (right) with an unknow visitor (left) at Giant Rock Spacecraft Convention

During his life, Barton published a series of booklets on different topics: *Flying Saucer Revelations, Venusian Health Magic, Venusian Secret-Science, Your D Day Destiny, D-Day Seers Speak, Secrets of Higher Contact, Rainbow City, and the Inner Earth People.*

Barton died on June 26, 2003 in Los Angeles, California.

The information and message presented in Barton's booklets appear sincere and genuine in feelings. But whatever was the metaphysical meaning of his writings: Barton was an important figure in UFO history.

It Will Happen In February!

by
Michael X

"IT WILL HAPPEN IN FEBRUARY!"

- By -

MICHAEL X

* * *

This is an Educational and Inspirational Course of Study... especially written and intended for NEW AGE Individuals everywhere. The following Seven Chapters are contained herein:

1. WHY ASTROLOGERS ARE IN A DITHER

2. WORLD WAR III IN FEBRUARY 1962?

3. WILL A NEW WORLD TEACHER APPEAR?

4. WILL THE FLYING SAUCERS RETURN?

5. WILL THE EARTH FLIP IN FEBRUARY?

6. HOW THIS CONJUNCTION AFFECTS YOU

7. YOUR "AQUARIAN RIGHT-ACTION" NOW

* * * * *

Statements in this Course are based on Scientific and Super-Sensory Findings. No claim is made as to what the information cited may do in any given case and the Publishers assume no obligation for opinions expressed or implied herein by the author.

FOREWORD

Dear New Age Friend:

In February, 1962, one of the most significant configurations of planets in the long history of mankind, is due to "happen" in the heavens. It is called, "The Great Conjunction" of 1962.

Important? Very. One writer on the subject says that an identically similar event hasn't occurred in over 25,000 years. However, I would bring down this figure considerably by suggesting it could have happened 600 years ago. For the astronomer Cassini discovered that it takes exactly 600 years (one Naros cycle) for our Sun and its planets to repeat an identical position in the heavens. In the coming conjunction five major planets Mercury, Venus, Mars, Jupiter and Saturn, plus our Sun and Moon, are involved.

Although conjunctions of 3 or more planets are not new -- they do occur with some regularity -- a Conjunction like that coming up in February deserves special consideration because it is a very heavy concentration of planets and because our world is going through a tense and critical phase of expression politically, internationally and spiritually, at this particular point in history.

Top astrologers have given considerable publicity to this forthcoming Great Conjunction. It has received world-wide attention by students of astrology, devotees of Philosophy, enthusiasts of prophecy, and...believe it or not..."hard-headed businessmen"! Why? That is the fascinating and tremendously vital theme of this book. You will soon find yourself caught up in the exciting, rewarding "NEW AGE ADVENTURE" of unravelling that theme.

Here, though, is a "clue". Those top astrologers expect some mighty dynamic occurrence under the five planets combining in an "all-star" performance in February. The big question is: WHAT?

I believe that if we look for unusual and sensational outer phenomena and only that, we are likely to be disappointed. Thrilling possibilities related to this coming stellar event inevitably "touch" the "inner" as well as the "outer" man. Let us keep this in mind as we, with the inspiration of the Wise Ones, prevue FEBRUARY, 1962!

MICHAEL X

"IT WILL HAPPEN IN FEBRUARY!"

Part 1

Why Astrologers Are in a Dither

You might as well know right off that I am not an Astrologer. I don't claim to know "all about the stars" nor, for that matter, all about anything. My profession is writing. I am a "New Age" writer.

But I do include in my circle of good friends some Astrologers who are long-time students of the art and science of "casting Horoscopes" and charting the stars.

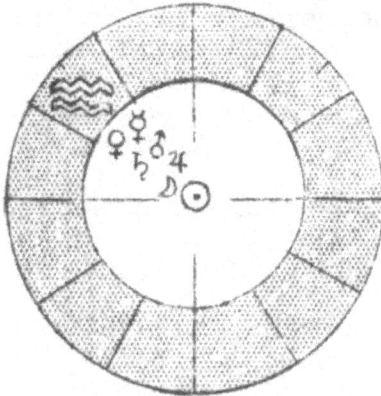

They have convinced me by now that there is a scientific basis for Astrology. I have -- with my own eyes -- seen many of their Horoscope predictions work out with uncanny accuracy. They have even taught me some of the rudiments of the art... how to chart the exact position of the various planets at the time of one's birth, and what kind of a temperament, character and life the individual might expect if born under the influence of a particular grouping of planets.

That is why I stood at respectful "attention" the day I first heard my Astrologer friends talk about the "Great Conjunction" of planets due to take place very shortly. In February, 1962. That is when the terrific event will occur. All good Astrologers know of it and, to say they are excited is putting it mildly indeed.

They are in a complete "dither" over it! Why? I shall, in this chapter, give you several reasons for their excitement over the impending Great Conjunction.

Before I list those reasons, though, perhaps I'd better give you a working definition of that word, "Conjunction", since it is an astrological term.

The word "conjunct" means joined together. A Conjunction then, refers to the apparent "joining together" of heavenly bodies in space. We say apparent because in a conjunction the planets actually do not meet nor join together at all. They only appear to. In reality, the planets line up in a row during a conjunction, and to an observer with a telescope they would seem to be "joined together". What really happens -- according to our Astronomers -- is that the planets are grouped together in a line in the same sign or constellation of stars.

Now this Great Conjunction we are talking about in this book will be made up of five major planets -- Mercury, Venus, Mars, Jupiter and Saturn. In Astrology, the Zodiac of the heavens is comprised of twelve "signs" or constellations, one of which is called Aquarius.

In the month of February, 1962, those five major planets will all enter the same 19-degree arc in the sign of Aquarius. The planets will begin "conjuncting" (conjoining) -- lining up together in a row -- as early as February first...and all five will have completed the Conjunction by February 5th. That is the basic picture.

It's an exciting one. Astrologers everywhere keep asking themselves the big question: what is going to happen? What event will accompany this Conjunction?

Recently, THE SUNDAY DESPATCH, London, England, had this to say:

"Top astrologers expect some mighty dynamic occurrence under the five planets combining in an all-star performance not due again for thousands and thousands of years..."

Here are a total of SEVEN possibilities that all of us ought to consider now in regard to the Great Conjunction due in February. These are the "reasons" why many astrologers are in a very real "dither" of excitement:

(1) World War III -- "Hot" style, could start. The astrologers say "could"; they don't say it will. None of us want to face this hellish possibility. It is far too horrible a thought, now that all the big nations of the world have atomic weapons, guided missiles, etc. But in spite of its gruesome unpleasantness the grim fact is: we've got to consider the possibility of such a war.

As I am writing this, President J. F. Kennedy has just given the "orders" to "beef-up" all of our national defenses on an unprecedented scale. The defense build-up will cost billions of dollars, and every man, woman and child in this United States of America is involved -- tax-wise and otherwise -- in this Defense Preparation Effort.

Triggering this action has been the "Berlin Crisis", the only situation big enough to possibly trigger a major war -- World War III -- in which America and the Soviet Union would battle it out together to a finish.

On top of this terribly touchy situation in Berlin, comes the Great Conjunction in February to add "fuel" to an already overheated international relationship. Will the world leaders crack under the added strain of planetary stress? Making matters still worse, as far as Man's peace of mind is concerned, there are some predictions going the rounds now, that 1962 IS THE YEAR when the atomic holocaust -- World War III -- will start!

(2) A Great World Teacher may appear.

This possibility -- the appearance of a Spiritual Messenger of Light and Truth -- in February of 1962, has many astrologers and vast numbers of esoteric students quite excited. All of these individuals are enthused.

Happily, there is a certain amount of valid reason for their enthusiasm as we shall explain further on. We shall, in fact, devote a whole chapter to the subject.

When those Higher Intelligences which guide the evolution of mankind have determined upon a specific ideal or principle which shall hold together in unity the minds of the human race for a period of time, a Teacher is sent.

(3) Spacecraft -- not of this world -- may suddenly return again in large numbers in our skies! The word is out: watch 1962. Unusual things are going to happen.

In spite of the fact that Flying Saucer Sightings have declined dramatically in the past few years, there are those who believe that the trend could reverse itself if there were a good reason for it.

If the Space People return in their amazing Space Ships there is certainly going to be a very good reason for them to do so. They will most certainly have some great message to get across to the humanity of earth... and it is not inconceivable that they, as Messengers of Light from far off kingdoms "not of this world" may herald the coming of a marvelous World Teacher..to earth.

- 5 -

(4) <u>Major Earthquakes</u> -- <u>big ones</u> -- <u>may</u> occur.

You -- the New Age individual -- have gasped with no small amount of trepidation when earthquakes, mighty quakes like the great Chile Quake, the Montana Yellowstone Quake, and the Agadir Quake and Tidal Wave occurred within very recent times.

Now, many people believe that the "electro-magnetic energies" released into our planet earth by the Great Planetary Conjunction of February, 1962, are going to be powerful enough to cause some <u>bad</u> earthquakes.

It is a scientific fact -- not fantasy -- that this massive planetary configuration in February brings with it terrifically positive, impelling pressures. Not only will these pressures -- invisible though they are -- exert definite, unusual force upon you and me and persons everywhere...they'll also put great pressures upon the geographical globe we live upon.

I don't wish to frighten you, but you ought to know that it is possible to accurately predict earthquakes in advance merely by knowing when Planetary Conjunctions are due. It seems that the massing of planets in one area causes extra stress on the earth. The faults in the substrata of the earth tend to readjust themselves under such stress. The result? Earthquakes!

(5) <u>Planet Earth's</u> <u>present</u> "<u>axis</u>" <u>might</u> <u>shift.</u>

Now earthquakes -- even severe ones -- are one thing. But the shifting of planet earth upon its axis is quite another thing. The possibility of such an event happening in February is not as remote as you might think at first glance and we ought to look further into the idea. We are, however, going to reserve that for another chapter.

(6) <u>Aquarian Influence</u> <u>will</u> be <u>felt</u> <u>by</u> <u>all.</u>

There is very little doubt about this possibility. Astrologers are certain that, beginning in February, the influence of Aquarius will touch every one of us deeply.

Aquarius has two big traits. Humanitarianism and extreme independence. It's an air sign, so we can look for tremendous "break-thru's" in our Space Exploration program. Earthman is going to push out much farther into "deep" space in 1962...with the aid of a new engine that

runs on atomic fuel. This new engine, plus plenty of new
ideas, will bring us more data on what is "out there"...

Watch how the Aquarian purpose asserts itself. A
new way of life based on new ideas -- tremendous new ideas
-- is about to "take hold" on our planet in February.

These new ideas of Aquarius are unusual. Outer space
will be the origin of many of these new concepts, which
are different in every way from the old "ideologies" of
the fast-fading Piscean Age. Aquarius has always symbolized humanitarianism, personal freedom and progress. I
am happy to say "spiritual progress" comes first under
this highly inspirational new sign of Aquarius. That is
why this Great Conjunction of February marks a Turning-
Point for all peoples on planet Earth, in their cyclic
journey to a better state!

(7) An Era of fabulous Prosperity could begin!

This is the seventh and -- for many persons -- the
happiest possibility of all. Prosperity, greater than
anything we've ever known, should begin under this Sign.

These then, are Seven dynamic possibilities which a
Planetary Conjunction -- especially one the size of that
coming in February -- could manifest under the liberating
influence of the constellation known as Aquarius.

It is true that astrologers are in a dither over the
great zodiacal event now impending, and with the above
Seven Possibilities staring them in the face..no wonder!

The astrologers, however, are by no means alone. I
have found that their concern is shared also by a great
many good folks who -- like myself -- are not astrologers.

We are, however, serious truth seekers. We want to
get at the bottom of things no matter how drastic or fore-
boding they may seem on the surface. We want to know. If
there is anything really "dire" about the forthcoming big
stellar event we want to know about it. And, if there
are joyous, happy, uplifting experiences in store for us
-- and I am confident there are -- we want to know about
those also. This, of course, means just one thing.

We ought to explore those Seven Possibilities.

ooo0OOO0ooo

"IT WILL HAPPEN IN FEBRUARY!"

Part 2

World War III in February 1962?

In this book I am not going to give you a big con-
glomeration of political facts and figures which deal
with our present international crisis. The newspapers,
magazines, radio and televis-
ion are already providing you
with that information.

What we are going to do
is to contribute a different
view of the very delicate and
touchy situation that faces
the United States, Germany
and Soviet Russia. We shall
take a good look at the possibility of a major shooting
war. And we shall size up
the general situation in the light of this forthcoming
Great Conjunction of February, 1962.

According to the astrologers, this Conjunction isn't
favorable to any of our present world leaders. Kennedy,
Krushchev, Konrad Adenauer, Pope John in Rome, Queen Eliz-
abeth, Chiang Kai-Shek...all of these persons will find
themselves under unusual stress in February due to the
position of the planets at that time.

The Horoscope of each one of these leaders is not
at all favorably "aspected" in relation to this impending
Conjunction. To put it frankly, that is not good. The
general effect will be that our world leadership is going
to be burdened with decisions which, at the time, will
seem extremely difficult to make.

Each One of these world leaders mentioned above, is
sure to find extreme difficulty in deciding important
matters, and it is not unlikely that one or more of them
may make wrong moves. Moves that could "upset the cart".

Now while this situation of burdened leadership is
going to make for some badly frayed "nerves" the world
over, there is not likely to be a major shooting war in
February. Why not? Because neither the U.S. nor Russia
want big war. Russia's policy is to grab as much as she

can just short of big war. All the while threatening us with cries of : "Nuclear war! Nuclear war!"

The U.S. policy is to stop Russia short of big war.

When, then, could war start? Will a showdown ever come, or will we all just go on talking and threatening?

As far as the "Berlin Crisis" goes, a showdown is highly unlikely. The fight will be one of words rather than bullets...Nerves, of course, will take a beating.

We've been used to thinking that Russia is a strong empire. Fact is, it is strong militarily...but it is weak economically. Right now, there happens to be a serious shortage of food in the Soviet Union. Krushchev is fully aware that war -- coming on top of a scarcity of food rations -- isn't likely to be well thought of.

Krushchev also knows full well another fact. That which he stands to gain by getting control of Berlin... and keeping the U.S. out of West Germany...is nothing compared to what he stands to lose by having us blow up all of Russia. War--any war--even a small war anywhere in Europe, but especially in Germany, would quickly turn into an atomic war and then all hell would break loose.

Showdown won't come from direction we are all looking in, but it could come from an action by East Germany to try to keep U.S. out of Berlin. If that action comes, war could start. If it should, it could "trigger" the war we can't even bear to think about -- World War III...!

Considering the above, the logical conclusion is: No "Hot War" now. None in February, in spite of those strong planetary pressures that will be affecting all world leadership at that time. It will be critical, yes, but as before, the "crisis" will blow over.

Not, however, before a lot of good people in West Germany -- 250,000 of them and more -- hold more of those "mass-meetings" in public to "blow off steam" at the Communist organizers in East Germany. But West German Chancellor Adenauer says the biggest crisis comes...later.

I trust that by now you are breathing more easily about the tense situation in Berlin, but before you get too complacent and too relaxed, I think we ought to look at some of the "War Predictions" that are going around now...and see what we can make of them.

In the year 1959 a blind Hindu by the name of Chakravarty of Benares, India, took it upon himself to publicize a sensational prediction. This prediction had been made by Chakravarty's master who was called Pravo Jagadbandhu.

Jagabandhu -- some 60 years previous -- had given out actual dates when "doom" in the form of furious global war would befall the great nations of the world. The furious battle was to be fought in 1960-62. It was to be so bad that the land, water and atmosphere of the entire world would become exceedingly poisonous.

According to Jagadbandhu, this Third and Final World War would openly start at the end of the Cold War. That was "pin-pointed" for 1960. World War III was supposed to slowly get under way and then, in 1962, it was to be most heavily destructive. Nearly all the great countries of the world would be severely affected.

Of course, this "World War III" was not going to be the end of everything. The merciful Lord -- said Pravo Jagadbandhu -- will partially spare all the countries for His own next play of Love and Peace. That saving action would be visible from 1965 onward.

Well, there is the prediction; but what are the facts? What has actually happened to date?

Firstly, World War III did not begin openly at the end of the Cold War. 1960 is long past, and we are now well into 1961 and fast approaching 1962. During this period of time we have lived through the Laos crisis and -- now -- the Berlin crisis. Still no "hot" war.

As we have seen, war even on a "limited" scale is apt to snowball into a nuclear war overnight. And then there would be "hell" to pay on both sides. Some 200 million human beings would -- quite suddenly -- die.

Icy cold fact is: threat of big nuclear war is more than just a flowery dream. I just finished reading a book, "AMERICA: TOO YOUNG TO DIE!" by Major de Seversky.

Major Alexander P. de Seversky made a prediction I think you ought to know about. He is the man of whom Gen. Douglas MacArthur said: "All of his statements, all of his predictions have been proved eternally right."

As Major de Seversky sees it, Russia's striking power is far superior to ours at this moment. Russia is steadily out-distancing us militarily. Unless we "get going", 1962 will be the most CRITICAL year in modern history. War started by Russia in 1962 could destroy us completely.

Of course we'd "strike back" at Russia. But the damage we'd inflict would be "acceptable" to them, even though it would be terrible from any point of view. To those men in the Soviet Union who are dedicated to the ideology of World Communism, such a victory wouldn't seem overly expensive. They'd "rule" the world.

Sobering thought is: Russia knows that Germany has now risen to great industrial prominence and economic prosperity in just ten short years after having 80 per cent of her industries destroyed in World War II. What the Germans did to "recover", thinks Russia, she also can do.

No mention is made by Major de Seversky, of the existence of "unidentified flying objects" in our skies...nor of the possibility of "interplanetary intervention" by the UFO People from other planets in case of big war.

WHAT NOSTRADAMUS SAYS

One of our most popular sources of information on coming events -- including wars -- is of course our old friend Michel Nostradamus, the Seer of France.

Nostradamus knew about Astrology and was doubtless aware of forthcoming planetary conjunctions. He was able to tell -- by use of superconscious powers -- whether or not an individual or a nation was destined for troubles.

The period 1960-65 was, as he viewed it, critical. But not nearly so critical and dangerous as the period 1995--2000 A.D. That will be the most critical time for humanity, according to the French Seer. Around 1999 we will see the dreaded World War III unleased, just as the old century is ebbing away! Here is his prediction:

> "When a fish pond that was a
>   meadow shall be mowed,
> Sagittarius being in the ascendant,
> Plague, Famine, Death by the
>   military hand..
> The Century approaches renewal."

Trying our hand at an interpretation, we note that "a fish pond" refers to the Piscean Age (Pisces: fish).

When the Piscean Age has come to its close, it is just like a "meadow that shall be mowed". At the turn of the Century the star constellation we call Pisces is -- astrologically speaking -- near its final ebb. Calculating it in time, it would be around 1999.

That is when -- according to Nostradamus -- a major war will come. How long will it last? Read on:

> "Fire shall fall from the skies
>   on the King's palace
> When Mars' light shall be eclipsed,
>   Great war shall be for
> Seven months, people shall die
>   by witchcraft,
> Rouen and Eureux shall not
>   fail the King."

Nostradamus predicts that this climactic "war of wars" will start when Russia invades Iran (not Berlin). This war between the reds and the whites -- as he terms them -- will terrify mankind until the seventh month of 1999 when the reds will lose and peace reigns at last. But note this carefully: peace will come, not because whites beat the reds, but because intelligent beings from another planet intervene on behalf of other worlds. Henry Roberts of New York (to whom we give credit for the interpretations in this paragraph) says that the first sign of these "space cadets" will appear just before the hydrogen bomb is perfected. Nostradamus said it. I think you'll agree that it happened. UFO appeared then.

World War III won't happen in February, 1962... thank God. But it is scheduled by Destiny to happen by 1999 unless wise men act smartly to avert it. That is a real possibility, as I see it.

The big thing that WILL HAPPEN in February is this: A dynamic "break-thru" of the Aquarian purpose which is strongly humanitarian, strongly FOR human liberty and freedom, strongly for ideals having to do with the higher well-being and progress of all peoples. I believe it is this very feeling -- released in a sudden magnified way by the Great Planetary Conjunction -- that will impel our world leaders to "hold back the dogs of war" in February.

oooOOOOooo

"IT WILL HAPPEN IN FEBRUARY"

Part 3

Will a New World Teacher Appear?

A number of religious faiths have long awaited the coming of a new World Teacher...a highly evolved Spiritual Master. In the past, our world has seen many such Teachers. Now, with the Great Conjunction due to occur in February, one of the biggest questions many persons are asking is:

Will a great new Teacher make his appearance during the month of February, 1962?

Before I give you my opinion as to that, let us take a quick look at some very unusual and important history. Follow me closely if you will, please. When the month of February rolls around, five planets, Mercury, Venus, Mars, Jupiter and Saturn, will enter into a "conjunction" together with the Sun and the Moon. Total of 7.

I wish to make it very clear that major conjunctions of 4, 5, or 6 planets are not too unusual. In the last 100 years, for example, there have been at least four conjunctions involving six planets. Three of those conjunctions preceded the outbreak of war: Civil War, Spanish American War, and World War II. But planetary conjunctions are not always associated with destructive occurrences.

Messengers of Light sometimes enter the earthly scene at the height of a conjunction of planets. In 577-574 B.C. when three planets entered a new sign together -- in conjunction -- Gautama Buddha was born, transforming the life of the eastern half of the world.

And in the period 10 B.C. to 30 A.D., when another conjunction of three planets occurred, Jesus was born. He transformed the life of the western half of the world. So we see it isn't the number of planets in the conjunction that is all-important, but the status and need of humanity. When a tremendous need exists -- when humanity is walking the "razor's edge" and about to fall, help is sent.

It's happened before. Earth's humanity has not been forsaken down through the ages. Not at all. In just the last few Millenniums we earthlings have enjoyed the amazing wisdom and "spiritual guidance" of a good many marvelously enlightened souls. World Teachers aren't something strange or new in our history..just look:

Zoroaster	Krishna
Hermes	Bala-Rama
Osiris	Vyasa
Horus	Akhenaten
Cadmus	Marduk
Orpheus	Buddha
Atys	Izdubar
Adonis	Witoba
Hammurabi	Appollonius of Tyana
Manu	Laotse
Mithras	Quetzalcoatl
Moses	Pythagoras
Dionysus	Plato
Hercules	Numa
Sargon	Confucius
Serapis	Yehoshua ben Pandira
Sabazius	Jesus
Tammuz	Mohammed

Each one of the above individuals had a specific job to do in "awakening" mankind into a progressively higher and more perfected state of awareness in body, mind and soul. Each came to assist a bewildered human race to see more of REALITY and less of ILLUSION. Each taught and proclaimed the TRUTH in a clear, positive way so that ERROR would cease ruling and retarding mankind.

When those Higher Intelligences which guide the evolution of mankind have determined upon that fixed ideal or principle most needed by Man for a certain epoch of time...in order that a definite range of experience may be gained by the human race...they send their Messenger to humanity. Spiritually, such a being is highly evolved. He is especially endowed with the radiance and life-giving powers of the God-Spirit so that its divine regenerative force may be poured forth from that person to everyone whom he contacts.

In this manner, a World Teacher "awakens" all humans and creates in their minds that NEW IDEAL which shall give a dynamic impulse to human evolution. When the purpose of that ideal is achieved, the Teacher with-

draws from the outer phase of the world scene. It is a
fact of great significance that planetary conjunctions
play a big role in the coming of every Great World Teacher. For example, consider the rise and fall of the
ancient Roman Empire. Under a certain conjunction the
first King of the Romans, Numa, came forth.

Numa, Son of the Sun, was sent as Messenger of
Light by those Higher Intelligences which guide mankind's
evolution. He imparted to early Roman civilization that
spiritual impulse and initiative which vitalized it in
its new ideals of strength and regeneration of the race.
But note this: Into that spiritual impulse was poured
extra "Sun Force" from the conjunction of planets -- dom-
inated by Mars -- under which the Roman civilization was
generated. When that force was withdrawn, the Empire declined. In fact, it collapsed. Numa was not remembered.

Another significant fact. Highly advanced beings
of "World Teacher" calibre are frequently sent to this
Earth from other planets in the universe. Planets that
are in harmony with universal laws of LIFE, LOVE, LIGHT.
Jesus, for example, admitted this, saying: "My kingdom
is not of this world."

A World Teacher could be born on this Earth in the
usual manner, grow up into adulthood, and then teach us.
But he doesn't necessarily have to follow that procedure.
Especially now. We earthlings are now living in the Last
Days of an Old Dispensation and Time is fast running out.

The "Second Coming" of the Master Jesus is not expected to take place before the turn of the century, but
many students of the UFO subject believe that he will
send certain "interplanetary delegates" to assist in the
awakening of earth people before the great event occurs.

One such Messenger of Light is an interplanetary
being known as ASHTAR-SHERAN. The word "Sheran" means
Commander, and Ashtar is said to hold the rank of Chief
Commander of the five Space Fleets of his home planet
Metharius. Metharius is located in the Alpha Centauri
system, some 4.3 light years from our planet Earth. It
is whispered in UFO circles that the spiritual influence
of Ashtar, as well as that of many other mighty Masters
of Light, will be especially active in FEBRUARY.

I want you to realize now, before the actual time
of the Conjunction arrives, that this event in February
will mark a "Spiritual Turning Point" for all of us.

oooOOOOOooo

"IT WILL HAPPEN IN FEBRUARY!"

Part 4

Will The Flying Saucers Return?

Interplanetarians -- that is, advanced human beings who are able to travel from planet to planet, from star to star -- by means of spaceships, are not figments of earthman's imagination. On the contrary, they are entirely real. They exist...whether the people of this earth realize it or not.

For years I have been shouting this truth to all those who were "awakened" enough mentally and spiritually to listen to me.

The books I have written on this subject number a good round "baker's dozen"...and I am still at it. My work is not yet completed. The job of "world UFO enlightenment" must continue, because this is part of a Great Cosmic Plan which is in action right now within our magnificent universe.

Back in 1957, I happened to read a brief article in the San Diego Union newspaper. I'd like to quote that article now, for the especial benefit of my new students who probably have never seen any interplanetary flying saucers and may not know quite what to "believe" regarding them. This information is right to-the-point.

SAUCER-TYPE SPACE OBJECTS REPORTED. Washington, Jan. 15, 1957 (A.P.) Rear Adm. Delmer S. Fahrney, USN, ret., once head of the Navy's guided missiles program, today said reliable reports indicate that "There are objects coming into our atmosphere at very high speeds."

Fahrney told a news conference that "no agency in this country or Russia is able to duplicate at this time the speed and acceleration which radar and observers indicate these objects can achieve."

Fahrney said he never has seen a flying saucer but has talked with a number of scientists and engineers who have reported seeing strange flying objects. He added there are signs that HUMANS are directing the objects.

- 16 -

"They are not entirely actuated by automatic equipment," he said. "The way they change position in formations and override each other would indicate that their motion is directed."

Two things I'd like you to note about that article. (1) Fahrney himself never saw a flying saucer. In spite of that lack of first hand experience, he is brave enough to recognize and admit that unknown objects were being sighted in our skies. Objects capable of speeds which none of the aircraft (or missiles) from any nation on this earth are able to match.

(2) The date of this article is 1957...the year of the last big "Saucer Flap" (Mass sightings) in the U.S.A.

One more bit of earthly "scientific opinion" and then we shall take up the colossal question: Will the flying saucers return in 1962?

In 1959, the Associated Press carried this highly significant statement by Professor Hermann Oberth, who was one of the experts at the German Rocket Station at Peenemunde on the Baltic Coast northeast of Berlin:

"I am convinced that the things called flying saucers are real and perhaps are manned by the 'Vikings' from another planetary system. We cannot produce such 'saucers' yet....Thus one concludes that these flying objects are the exploring ships of another solar system, or even of a far-off fixed star."

What these hard-headed scientific men are saying is essentially this: The UFO's or flying saucers are real. They are coming from other planets in outer space and the human beings who pilot those spaceships are far ahead of the people of earth in technical progress.

Now let's get at that big question: Will the Flying Saucers return in 1962? In order to predict the future we have one great factor to go by. Past performance. If we know what kind of a showing the "Saucers" have made during the past 15 years, it ought to indicate to us some trend or "cyclic pattern" which could guide us in our efforts to mentally project forthcoming events.

I'd like you to study the Chart on the next page carefully. It shows the frequency of UFO sightings. Note, however, that only U.S.A. sightings are listed. World-wide, at least 70,000 persons have seen UFO's.

- 17 -

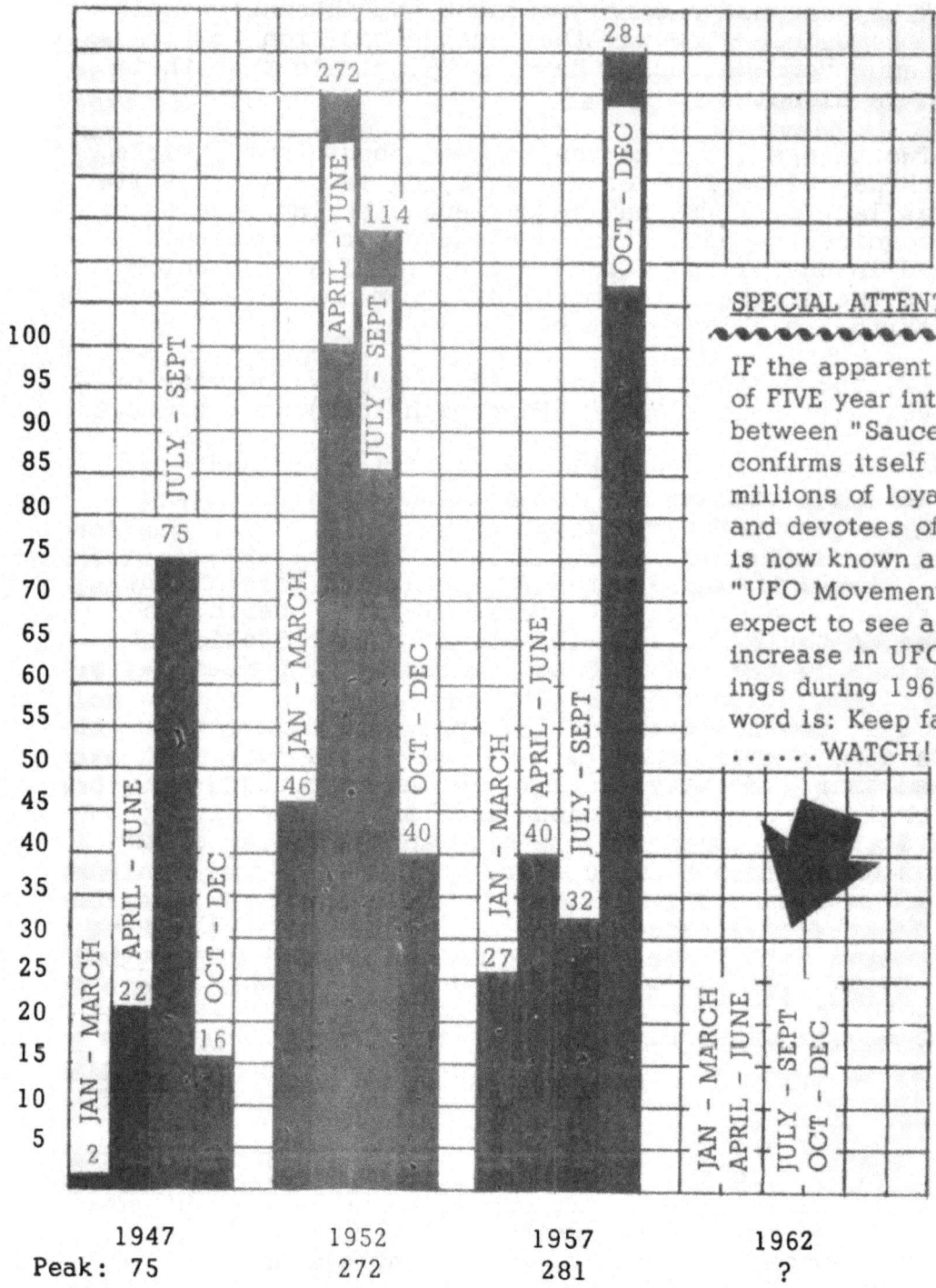

SPECIAL ATTENTION:

IF the apparent "trend"
of FIVE year intervals
between "Saucer Flaps"
confirms itself in 1962,
millions of loyal fans
and devotees of what
is now known as the
"UFO Movement", can
expect to see a positive
increase in UFO sight-
ings during 1962. The
word is: Keep faith and
......WATCH!

Chart data:

1947 — Peak: 75
- JAN – MARCH: 2
- APRIL – JUNE: 22
- JULY – SEPT: 75
- OCT – DEC: 16

1952 — Peak: 272
- JAN – MARCH: 46
- APRIL – JUNE: 272
- JULY – SEPT: 114
- OCT – DEC: 40

1957 — Peak: 281
- JAN – MARCH: 27
- APRIL – JUNE: 40
- JULY – SEPT: 32
- OCT – DEC: 281

1962 — Peak: ?
- JAN – MARCH
- APRIL – JUNE
- JULY – SEPT
- OCT – DEC

FREQUENCY CHART OF UFO SIGHTINGS IN THE LAST 15 YEARS

Note: Only U.S.A sightings, reported to Govt., are listed.

Now if you have studied the Chart closely, you are sure to have noted an unusual fact. The frequency or periodicity of Flying Saucer Sightings over the last 15 years shows a rather marked 5 year Cycle. Mass-sightings known as "Saucer Flaps", appear to have occurred in regular intervals of five years:

YEAR	PEAK
1947	75
1952	272
1957	281
1962	?

Five year cycles! Do we have a trend? Might we expect another "Saucer Flap" to occur in 1962, and a great international upsurge of interest in the subject of Interplanetary Visitations by people from other planets?

Quite possible. I might even say, highly probable. But lest we make the serious mistake of "throwing all caution to the winds" and reaching wrong conclusions, I must add: not necessarily. We may NOT have a trend. It takes more than 3 consecutive cycles to constitute a true trend, and you will notice that to date we have only 3 cycles.

We do, however, have a definite "indication" of a genuine trend. If the cyclic pattern continues good, and mass sightings suddenly occur in 1962, then we have a predictable trend which every Saucer devotee ought to find very valuable for future forecasts. It's reasonable to expect the return of ASHTAR'S FLEET in '62. KEEP ALERT!

IS THERE ANY REASON FOR THE 5-YEAR CYCLES?   Can the apparent 5-year intervals between mass-sightings of UFO's be explained? Here is one explanation I have heard that could be correct. We know that UFO's have various points of origin -- have come from different places. But the biggest fleet seems to be coming from our nearest Star Alpha Centauri, 4.3 light years away.

Traveling at the speed of light, a space ship from Alpha Centauri would reach earth in 4 years and 3+months. Assuming it stayed 8+months to "look us over", 5 years would have elapsed. A Fleet of UFO's may have left earth in 1957 to return to home planet, while a new Fleet could arrive in 1962!

oooOOOOOooo

"IT WILL HAPPEN IN FEBRUARY"

Part 5

Will The Earth Flip in February?

As you and I now realize, the month of February in the year 1962, is the big month to watch. It is going to be a month in which a very "heavy" massing of planets in the sign of Aquarius, will occur. So concentrated is the massing of planets in one area of the heavens that we are justified in referring to the situation as a "Conjunction".

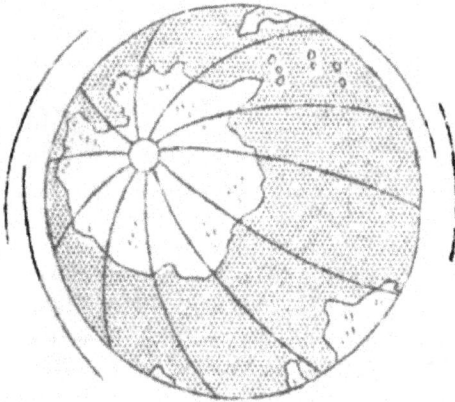

Now it is a fact -- discovered around 1935 -- that Planetary Conjunctions are frequently capable of causing earth QUAKES or tremors of considerable magnitude, when all factors are right. If this is true, then the next question that logically follows is: Will the Conjunction in February, '62, subject the earth to such stress that the world will shift on its axis? Is such a "polar flip" imminent?

Before we attempt to answer, I think we ought to establish at least some evidence that "polar flips" have really occurred in the past history of the earth. That will put us on fairly "solid" ground from which we shall tackle the urgent matter of our immediate future.

Here, then, is vital new evidence:

NEW EVIDENCE SHOWS ANTARCTIC ONCE WARM. Washington, Feb. 6, 1960 (UP) - Soviet scientists have reported discoveries which suggest that now-frozen Antarctica was a fertile continent 200 to 300 million years ago.

Together with findings of other scientists, the new evidence indicates that the South Pole continent was warm once and received considerably more sunlight than it gets now. This suggests to some scientists that the various continents shifted their relative positions on the earth's face in the remote past, or that there was a CHANGE in the planet's AXIS OF ROTATION. (Comment by M.X. - It is high time the possibility was admitted by science!)

- 20 -

Ten kinds of spores, proving past existence of fern-like plants, plus unidentified fragments of plant tissue were discovered in ancient Antarctic rock formations believed to be 200,000,000 to 300,000,000 years old.

Scientists here were interested in the Russian report but took exception to the Soviet claim that Russia was the first to discover plant remains near the South Pole. It was recalled that Swedish explorers found traces of ancient vegetable matter in Antarctica back in 1901.

Dr. Lucy M. Cramwell of New Zealand last year reported evidence -- perhaps 60,000,000 years old -- that forests once grew in Antarctica like those now common in southern South America.

Dr. George Llano, American lichenologist who has done research in Antarctica, said this evidence and the existence of coal in Antarctica indicated the continent got more sunlight in times past than it does now. Coal beds are fossilized vegetation. Such vegetation had to have lots of sunlight to live and thrive. -- Chicago Trib.

So it did happen before. A "polar flip". Or, at the very least, a tremendous shifting of huge continents. And if it happened before...it could happen again!

Just recently I received a most interesting letter from my friend Victor Filewood of Connecticut. Mr. V. Filewood made a study of astrology under the noted astrologer Wynn (Sydney K.Bennett) and has a good knowledge of the subject. With his kind permission, I now reprint some excerpts from his letter, regarding Earth's "next flip":

A MOST IMPORTANT   Dear Michael: First, neglecting
LETTER REVEALING   the Astrological and esoteric implica-
VITAL INFORMATION   tions, look at the "mechanics" of such
                          a Conjunction. I believe that Newton's
Law of Gravity states that: Bodies attract each other in
direct ratio to their weight and mass; and inversely as
the square of their distance apart.

"The more 'bodies' concentrated in one small sector of the Zodiac -- the greater will be the mutual attraction between them and our earth. No? Using this law, a scientific Astrologer named Reuben Greenspan found that he could accurately predict EARTH-QUAKES by merely using an Ephemeris (guide-book of planet positions) to know when planets would conjunct and thus cause extra stress on

- 21 -

earth. The "faults" in the sub-strata would tend to readjust under such stress. Result: Earthquakes.

"Now place five planets in one small area (19 ≈≈ -- Aquarius -- 19th degree) and how much unusual "pull" will there be? To this add the fact (claimed) that earth's axis is already "wobbling" from tremendous excess of ice off-center at the South Pole.

"Many scientists and others expect that the earth will "roll over like a pumpkin in a pond". This would not only give us a new axis, but would fulfill the biblical prediction of a "New Heaven and a new earth"..since it would probably take ages for men to re-locate the "signs of the Zodiac" from their new orientation.

"Keep up your good work. I enjoy your writings (the Michael X publications) It looks to me as though we are in for a rough time BEFORE the happy prophecies can be fulfilled. Perhaps I am too pessimistic about this angle. The new axis does nôt have to occur, but I believe it will.

"A five-planet Conjunction could precipitate this. That is the point I was trying to make, Have neglected mentioning the spiritual significances. You and others are covering that, in excellent manner. Sincerely, Vic."

COMMENTS BY MICHAEL X:

I know my good friend Victor Filewood will forgive me when I state that -- with all due respect to his opinion -- I do not anticipate Earth's axial shift in February. I do, however, agree with him on several basic points. One: Earth will be subjected to unusual stress during the conjunction. Two: Earth has "flipped" before.

My own researches have taught me that "axial shifts" of the earth have occurred in the dim past. The most recent shift of the poles occurring not 200,000,000 years ago as the Russians think...but only 7,000 years ago.

According to some of the world's most ancient teachings about earth's cycles, a shifting of the poles takes place on a regular basis once every 7,200 years. Since it is true that mankind is now nearing the end of such an epoch of time, it is not too much fantasy to expect that a similar "Great Event" may happen once more. The big question "How soon?" resolves itself into the knowledge of just two main factors: (1) How close are we to the end of the 7,200 year Epoch of Time, (2) How great an electromagnetic stress is created by the Conjunction of February, 1962.

For light on the first unknown factor, I turn again to an old friend Edgar Cayce, the famous clairvoyant or "Seer" of Virginia Beach, Virginia.

When Cayce was asked in 1938: "What great change or beginning of what change, if any, is to take place in the earth in the year 2000 to 2001 A.D.?", he replied,

"When there is a shifting of the poles. Or a new cycle begins."

If Cayce is correct on this score, we have about 38 years to go (figuring from 1962) before the next polar shifting is due. By that time, earth's scientists will no doubt, have arranged for a great "air-lift" of all the people by means of some new type of aircraft. We will all "take to the skies" during the shifting and be returned safely to the earth when all is well. I would prefer this method to the "underground tunnel" idea.

A few years ago, there was a real danger that the earth would do a sudden polar flip prematurely -- ahead of Destiny's regular schedule. The earth planet had developed a serious "wobble" that was a menace to our safety. Cause of the condition was undoubtedly the constant explosive testing of atomic bombs since 1945.

Now the mere exploding of an A-bomb does not jar the planet enough to cause it to begin wobbling. What really takes place is this. Earth's North Pole is negative and the South Pole is positive. Explode an A-bomb and gigantic quantities of "negative ions" are released into the atmosphere as "fallout".

Those negative particles are attracted by the earth's positive South Pole! As the particles fall to earth, they gather moisture -- rain or snow -- and of course it all falls on the South Polar area. A massive build-up of ice then occurs at the Pole, or rather "off-center" from the Pole..so that the added weight gradually starts an eccentric motion or wobble of the globe.

Four-fifths of the world's ice, my friend, according to the modern geo-physicists, is at the South Pole! That is why continued "nuclear testing" of atom bombs is suicidal as far as earth's balance is concerned. Too much ice build-up at the South Pole could "trigger" a polar shift faster than anything else.

I believe the "UFO People" knew of our peril and did miraculous things to stabilize our planet and keep it from "flipping" out of its orbit. That was a major part of their mission to earth. The danger of earth doing a polar flip now is over in my opinion. Thanks to "their" magnificent assistance spiritually and scientifically.

If -- however -- the big nations of earth ever take the final step of idiocy and unleash a full-scale nuclear war, the danger of a polar flip at once becomes 1000% greater. A danger of that degree, affecting as it would, not only earth and its humanity, but other planets within the solar system also, could not be permitted.

The day that earthman takes the step to such destruction would be the signal for "X-Day"...the Day when the UFO people would concentrate all their combined power upon this earth, and if need be, land their Space Fleets here.

As to the second factor we are curious about: How great an electromagnetic stress will be created by the Conjunction in February? ... We find that the various planets involved in this Conjunction are not all in perfect orb of each other. Some are a few degrees out of a perfect line...and this cuts down the influence to some extent. There is, however, still a tremendous stress or pressure exerted because of the heavy grouping of planets in one small sector of the sky.

Then too, in the month of February there will be TWO eclipses, a Total Eclipse of the Sun and one of the Moon. These eclipses, together with the massing of the planets in Aquarius, could -- and most likely will -- "trigger" earthquakes during the critical month of February.

"At certain times," says Reuben Greenspan in his article: Planets, Gravitation and Earthquakes, "the Moon in its passage around the earth, comes into conjunction, i.e., lines up with another planet, whose mass is great enough to cause an appreciable increase in the Moon's pull on the earth. Should the conjunction take place over the meridian of a point on the earth's surface that has a crustal fault, it can be seen that this fault would be subjected to an unusual stress...We also know that earthquakes are movements of the Earth's crust, which is normally in a

- 24 -

state of rest, but sometimes owing to forces acting under
definite but as yet unknown laws, the state of equilib-
rium of the Earth's crust is upset.

"The tremendous force of gravity, particularly when
the combined gravitational forces of two astronomical bodies are concentrated on some point on the Earth's surface
where a fault exists, results in an earthquake.

"That earthquake's intensity depends on the mass of
the bodies, their distance from each other and the Earth,
and the weakness of the Earth's crust or strata at the
point where this combined or unusual force is concentrated."
--Reuben Greenspan, WYNN'S ASTROLOGY MAGAZINE, Jan. 1936.

Now my friend, earthquakes may not mean very much to
you if you've never had any first-hand personal experience
with them. As long as quakes, tidal waves, fires and so
forth take place in a remote part of the world...where you
or I are not immediately affected...we aren't concerned
too much. We just read the "news item" and forget it.

But if ever we go through a bad earthquake..that is
a different story. Then it strikes home. Like the man
said: "It hits us where we live." Then we are interested!

You may think: "It could never happen to me!" But
the fact is, our entire continent of North America is well
circled by Major Earthquake Zones. Did you know that?

California, of course, "takes the cake". It has a
Major Fault Line running vertically from the ocean into
Cape Mendocino, and another one -- the San Andreas Fault
--running laterally all the way from San Francisco through
San Diego. Here in Los Angeles I am sitting at this very
moment right smack on top of that gigantic Fault Line.

The September 1961 issue of FATE Magazine carried an
exciting report on the present condition of the San Andreas
Fault. Title of it was: "A DATE WITH DEATH". Since it
was in the nature of a prediction, I shall give you the
gist of it here. A great EARTHQUAKE is due for the several million residents of metropolitan Los Angeles.

This shocking information was obtained by Peter Hopkirk
of the London Daily Express through an interview with Prof.
Hugo Benioff of California Institute of Technology. No
punches were pulled by the Professor. "There is no doubt,"
he stated, "that Los Angeles is soon going to be struck by

- 25 -

a very severe earthquake. It will almost certainly kill hundreds of people and do terrible damage. There is absolutely nothing we can do...It could happen at any time. It is already overdue."

The San Andreas fault, according to the Professor, is some 15 miles deep and 2,000 miles long. Every year the earth on one side of the fault moves northward two inches, and that on the other side moves southward the same distance. The land -- at the fault itself -- isn't moving. It's dead still, but building up enormous pressures. It is bound to slip soon...then, WATCH OUT!

In 1933 Los Angeles suffered a light earthquake in which about 20 persons lost their lives and several hundred were injured. A few buildings collapsed.

The next quake -- the one long overdue -- will put that 1933 shocker to shame, by comparison. Its intensity would be a thousand times stronger, in the opinion of Prof. Hugo Benioff. Let's see now. If 20 persons were killed in 1933 by that quake, some 20,000 persons are due for a sudden demise in the next one....200,000 injured.

Why don't people in L.A. know about the danger? It would be bad publicity -- says Benioff -- "It could and probably would halt the present mass migration into the area."

The secret, at any rate, is out. I most certainly agree with Prof. Benioff that a super-quake is already overdue for L.A. It could happen this very minute. Or it could conveniently wait until additional stress like that from the Great Conjunction in February 1962 is placed on the Earth's crust. That stress might just be the one "straw that broke the camel's back" and that sets off the big slip of California's touchy San Andreas fracture.

On the other hand, it might not. None of us as yet know enough about the gravitational effect of planets on each other besides their effect on the Earth. Strange as it may seem, less is known about planetary effects on the earth than is known about those effects on Man.

Summing up, we'd say: no real danger of a "polar flip" in February. Earthquakes? Some in scattered areas of the globe. Los Angeles? "No man knoweth save the creative forces", but I am with Benioff...a BIG QUAKE is overdue. Let's see, how far away is that Conjunction???

oooOOOOooo

- 26 -

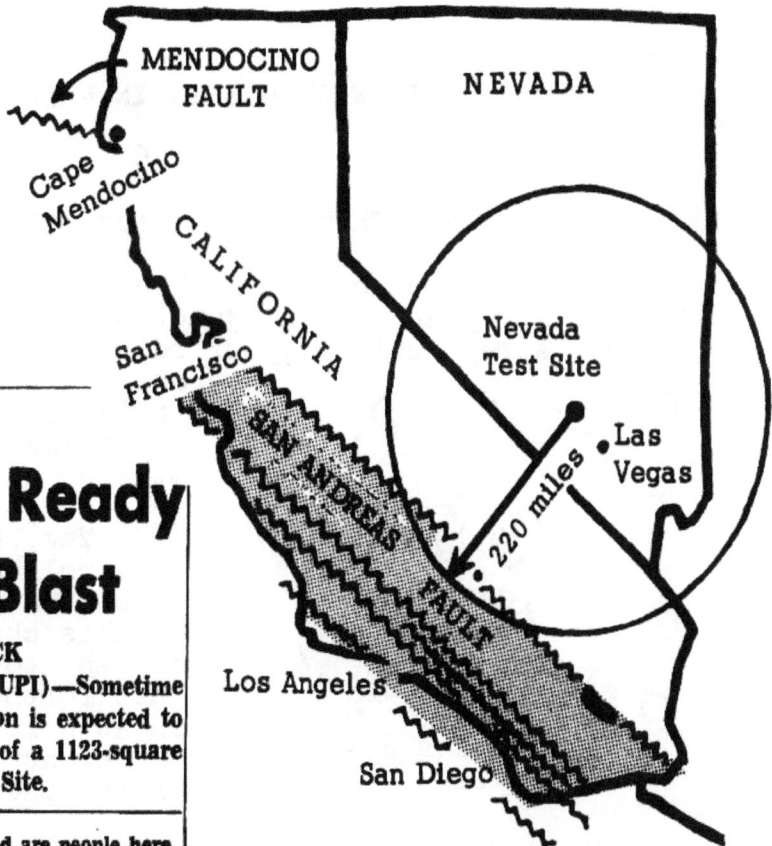

MENDOCINO FAULT

NEVADA

Cape Mendocino

CALIFORNIA

San Francisco

SAN ANDREAS FAULT

Nevada Test Site

220 miles

Las Vegas

Los Angeles

San Diego

TEST SITE IS 65 MILES FROM LAS VEGAS
Some Test Tunnels Reach 1½ Miles Into Rocky Mesas; First Tests to Be Comparatively Small

Expect Shot in 30 Days

Nevada Site Ready For Nuclear Blast

By ROBERT W. FLICK

RAINIER MESA, Nev., Sept. 6 (UPI)—Sometime this month an underground explosion is expected to jar this mesa nestled in the center of a 1123-square mile area known as the Nevada Test Site.

A small cloud of sand will be whipped up into the air. The effects of the blast four years ago has still not worn off.

This is the most logical underground test site since it is already very well equipped. It is a beehive of activity.

NO RADIATION

Touched off will be the sixth underground nuclear explosion in the history of the United States. There will be no flash. There will be no sound and no release of radiation into the atmosphere.

If there has been an exact date set for the test, only a few top-level Atomic Energy Commission members know it. And they are not talking. In fact, so tight-lipped are people here that even bartenders only nod.

President Kennedy, in announcing the lifting on a moratorium on nuclear tests yesterday, said a resumption of underground and laboratory tests would come within 30 days. Earlier, AEC spokesmen said such tests could be resumed within three weeks of a decision to go ahead.

2000 TNT TONS

The first underground shot was set off Sept. 19, 1957. Called Rainier, it was detonated at a spot about 900 feet below the top of the mesa in a tunnel. The blast, equal to nearly 2000 tons of TNT, was contained in a cavity about 120 feet in diameter.

Spokesmen said 5000 tons of rock about the ground zero point were pulverized and heat and pressure produced for a few seconds a glass ball which upon cooling returned to rock.

So intense was the heat produced by the rainier shot, one of 103 full scale explosions conducted here between Jan. 27, 1951 and Oct. 30, 1958, that today areas near ground zero maintain temperatures in excess of 110 degrees. Slight radioactivity is still present in the cavern.

Los Angeles Herald & Express
Wednesday, Sept. 6, 1961

SINCE President Kennedy gave the order for the U. S. to resume nuclear tests underground, we face a new danger. Such tests might trigger off the Earthquake Fault lines in California. Just how great this danger really is no one apparently can say. We do know that the Nevada A-bomb testing site is about 220 miles distant from the San Andreas Fault lines. Underground shocks equal to 2000+ tons of TNT aren't likely to help the earthquake hazard. Modern man is ignoring the lesson of Atlantis. We are told it was man, and not the forces of nature, that destroyed Atlantis. Or rather, men developed to such a degree their subterranean storehouses of electrified air, that the earth at last revolted and pitched man and his empire into the sea. The Big Question: Is history about to repeat itself in our time?

- 26-A -

"IT WILL HAPPEN IN FEBRUARY!"

Part 6

How This Conjunction Affects You

No question about it. You will be affected. This forthcoming planetary Conjunction in February is certain to make a real stir in your relationships with others... and it is going to stir your thoughts, feelings and actions like they've never been stirred before.

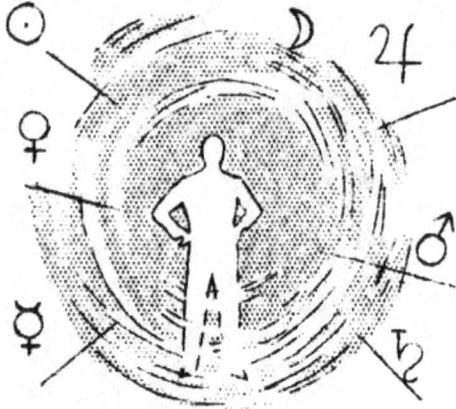

Yes, when February of 1962 rolls around, it brings with it a dynamic condition. In this chapter I am going to attempt to summarize for you that forthcoming condition . in as practical and helpful a manner as I can. Here, then, is the picture as it appears.

No World War III in February! In spite of the fact that the Berlin crisis has been and still is the gravest situation our world has faced since the "Cold War" began, it is not likely to culminate in a big war in February.

Why not? Because Aquarius is the "friend of the world" and not its enemy. This sign, Aquarius, radiates genuine, expansive, out-going friendliness. It's traditionally humanitarian. That is why it is highly unlikely that sudden death by nuclear warfare will be initiated during February.

Ideas, though, on both sides, are sure to be terrifically strengthened by the influences of the sign of Aquarius. The two ideologies, now opposing each other in the form of Soviet Communism and Western Democracy, will "battle it out" on a mental and emotional level as never before. But the conflict won't be physical.

Quite true, 1962 will be THE "Year of Decision" for World Leaders, just as it will be for you and me and the fellow next door. World leaders could -- under the extra stress caused by the planetary conjunction in February -- lose their balance and force destructive events to manifest "world-wide" just by impulsive decisions.

Aquarius, however, will be "pulling on our side" to such a degree that the tendency to wrong decisions does not seem to be strong enough to have the upper hand. I therefore look for a harmonious beginning in '62. The remainder of the year (1962) is another matter.

With no Big War in February, your life will not be threatened by atomic disintegration, so although you're likely to be busier than you've been in years...a dynamic new feeling of "extreme independence" and "self-reliance" will settle upon you. You'll notice it and be happy.

The preponderance of major planets in Aquarius during the Great Conjunction should have another effect, too. Expansiveness. Watch for it. You will feel as though a heavy weight has been lifted at last from your shoulders. This, as far as you are concerned is definitely good. It is no great crime to carry your share of the load as you travel the thrilling Pathway of Life, but when such burdens weight you down so much that you cease progressing, then it is high time you "tossed them off".

Liberation, then, is the keynote of Aquarius. And what liberates man more than anything else? Ideas -- do they not? So long as they are useful, helpful, illuminating to you and me and the neighbors next door.

Watch for ideas to flow into your mind much more freely and easily in February. Good ideas. You'll take them one at a time and "idealize" them by completing each detail of those ideas -- in line with Life's Spiritual Purpose -- and "presto", your ideas will have become Ideals to serve and guide you from day to day throughout 1962.

A Planetary Conjunction never fails to express itself in the mental, physical and emotional planes of the personal ego. In other words, the individuality of you receives a vibratory "modulation" -- a raising or lowering of vibrations, according to the intrinsic nature of the planets involved in the Conjunction.

Mercury, Venus, Mars, Jupiter and Saturn along with a Solar Eclipse (Feb. 4-5) will produce a combined modulatory vibration that is decidedly uplifting to you. Of especial significance is the Solar Orb in Eclipse. The Sun is the principle of life. Life unites. Hence a unifying effect will be manifested during that Eclipse. An effect which should -- along with the general Aquarian friendliness -- help to ease the international tensions.

- 28 -

Next thing to note is this. Although man's control and "domination" over other men will slacken in February, Nature's cosmic law of balance will not slacken. It is very likely to increase it's action of removing the unfit so that the true "New Age" Humanity can march forward to a smoother and faster rhythm.

Earthquakes, tremors and shocks are in the overall picture for the year 1962. Watch for them. If I am not badly mistaken, intensity of some of these quakes will be greater than 5 on a Richter seismograph which scales to 10.

Fundamentally this Great Conjunction in February is going to affect your general habits of life, because it is going to influence your thinking...considerably.

Aquarius has always symbolized humanitarianism, personal freedom and unusual new ideas. It is these new ideas that will suddenly start pouring into your "awareness" during the time of the Conjunction. Result? You'll find yourself stepping into a new way of life overnight.

A new way of life based on new ideas, tremendous new ideas of great simplicity, efficiency and the Aquarian purpose (Humanitarianism and extreme independence) is about to "take hold". You will enjoy it. But you must keep pace with it, for it is a new "acceleration".

Come February you will see the beginning of dynamic almost unbelievable changes. For one thing, President Kennedy's program of national defense and outer space exploration will produce many real and far-reaching changes. And those changes are certain to touch you "where you live" regardless of your age or occupation.

Making required changes won't be easy. They never are. Big key to making the changes with least amount of soul-stirring emotion and pain is...world-thinking. The future of the whole world is deeply involved in humanity's "decisions" in February. Our safeguard lies in a basic reversal of the Piscean attitude of "every man for himself". Our thinking must expand to include all beings.

Nostradamus and Edgar Cayce both agree that the period 1960-65 is not going to be nearly as bad as that period later on between 1995 and 2000 A.D. So we needn't be unduly concerned about our world ending in 1962 by nuclear war, nor by a planetary "shifting of the axis". It will be a disturbing year...but you will survive it.

ooooOOOOooo

"IT WILL HAPPEN IN FEBRUARY"

Part 7

Your Aquarian "Right Action" Now

Action equals reaction. We get out of a thing just what we've been willing to put into it. No more and no less. I mention this basic law because it applies here.

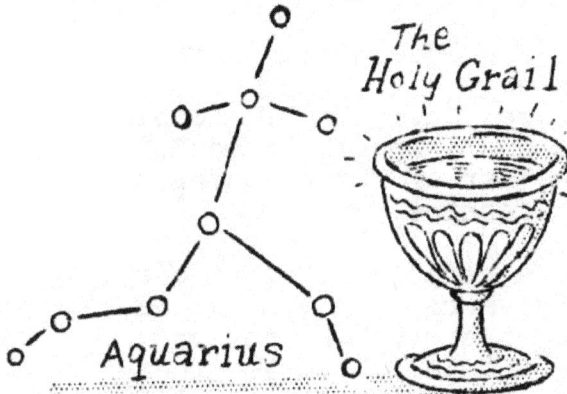

In a subject as big as this one we have been dealing with -- the Great Conjunction of planets in February -- it is childishly easy to "read things into" the event. We can, if we try hard enough, see all kinds of strange things happening during the planetary conjunction.

The Holy Grail

Aquarius

But we don't want to do that. We have enough solid data, statistical information and actual facts to go on, that I believe you will agree that we ought to stick to realities as closely as we can in "analyzing" the meaning and possibilities of the Conjunction.

You'll seldom find anybody any more audacious and adventurous than I am, dear reader, but I try to be logical as well as enthusiastic. I think we get farther when we look at things from more than one angle, with the idea of getting at the "inner truth" -- the "message" -- of what we are studying. I believe you agree with me.

Now this Great Conjunction that's coming up soon is a very solid, real "stellar event" that is definitely going to take place. That event, in itself, is unusual enough. Marvelous enough, too. Stop and think -- it's going to be a real "break-thru" for the Aquarian purpose. And unless I miss my guess terrifically as far as YOU are concerned, you've been longing, yearning and hoping for years for a bigger world acceptance of "NEW AGE" ideals. Well, February of 1962 will inspire Humanity.

1961 has been a year of political uprisings and rev-olutions. 1962 from February on, will be a year of new revelations for mankind. Men will start seeing things in a new light and "Ideologies" will begin to clash anew.

- 30 -

The elements of nature are not -- in my opinion --
going to "sit idle" during this new year facing us.
Planet Earth is going to struggle quite fiercely with
the elements in 1962 -- with the wild winds, floods, up-
heavals and quakings of the Earth in many places.

To those of you who happen to be long-time "Saucer
Devotees" and who still watch the skies for signs of the
heavenly ships from space, in spite of the general de-
cline in UFO sightings, I want to say this:

Do not feel that "they" -- the UFO People -- have
deserted you...that they are never going to return. I
want to most emphatically reassure you. The UFO People
never forsake their "own". You and I and the humanity
of this Earth have not seen the last of those wonderful
beings and their magnificent spaceships.

They'll be back. Their work here is far from over.
They've told me that. Also they've recorded the vibra-
tional wavelength of each one of the "true believers".
This will enable them to attune themselves to you when-
ever such attunement best serves the Great Cosmic Plan.

Meanwhile, right-action now is important. And that
means nothing less than "Aquarian" Right-Action. This
closely impending Quintuple Conjunction of planets in the
sign of Aquarius, demands action of minds and bodies.

The best time for action of course, is now. Before
February rolls around you will -- if you act now -- be
inwardly attuned and prepared for anything Destiny may
place upon your individual Doorstep. You'll be alerted
and ready also to make the best use of the dynamic new
spiritual impulse that is to be given to human evolution.

Let's be specific. What are the Five Things every
intelligent soul like yourself can do before February?

(1) Adjust. I think that you -- as a New Age Individual -- fully realize that the Universe in which you live
is not "standing still". It is evolving. It is progressing moment by moment into a finer, nobler, more "perfected" condition. And it is taking you and all of us right
along with it. And what does that signify?

Astrologically speaking, it signifies big changes.
From February on, through 1962, your life and the lives
of those persons who have been unduly troubled and dis-

- 31 -

tressed are going to be happier. You will be given more opportunity to work and to achieve, and this very fact will make you feel more secure. Financially, 1962 should be much better than usual for you...IF you "adjust" now to this new vibration of Aquarius. Here is how:

In Astrology, fire and air signs are positive...in contrast to earth and water signs which are negative. A positive sign such as Aquarius, which is an air sign, is apt to influence towards extremes of over-action. It contains within it an impulse to action...even to unbalance through excess. For this very reason, the month of February is certain to be a critical time for humanity, since an extreme of over-action on part of war-minded nations could plunge us into war on a major scale.

Realizing this "trait" of Aquarius (over-action) we recommend to you the practice of using your energies in the direction of Compensation...balancing up the books... paying off all debts to Nature and our fellow humans.. devoting extra thought to others...acting deliberately.

(2) Accept. This refers to changes. Accept them in the right spirit and that means of course, with gratitude for the new opportunities these changes will mean.

You'll see changes in home and apartment construction, in heating, lighting, television, entertainment, automobiles, planes, boats and so forth. Nobody can stop these changes. They're inevitable in a growing society.

Pain, though, comes from habit of "clinging" to the old ways...not expanding our vision to take in the NEW.

Attitude of "accepting" the new and better things of life (genuinely better, not "booby-traps") will help you avoid needless pain which, though mental, is pain nonetheless. Practice this. It's simple but essential.

(3) Advance. By getting yourself in step with cosmic, planetary and economic changes before February rolls around, you are going to be far more successful and far happier than you might otherwise be. Reason? Your new awareness. Your more positive habits. Your inward assurance that a "new way of life" is unfolding for you and for your fellow travelers on Life's Path.

Now I am positive that you have plans, desires, or causes that you are eager to realize in the new year.

You wouldn't be human if you didn't. Big question is: How can you best advance your own causes before February as well as afterward? To answer this rightly we have to take into full consideration the forthcoming planetary configuration, The Great Conjunction.

It boils down to this. In every battle which man wages (individually or collectively) against the "will of heaven" and higher progress, man is sure to lose. The all-embracing spiritual purpose at work in our Universe is simply too big..too strong. No man can beat it. In the long run it will always win.

Humanitarianism, service to others, reaching ever upward, like the eagle in flight, to bring constantly greater freedom and creative opportunity to all men... this, I am convinced, is inherently right and "in tune" with the will of heaven.

The secret then, is to advance your plans in line with this oncoming Aquarian purpose--thus advancing the "General Good"--and success is sure.

(4) Keep Poised. No use kidding ourselves or minimizing what is just ahead for humanity on this planet. February of 1962 is going to be a critical period for most of us. Planetary pressures -- electromagnetic in nature -- are bound to be greater than normal during that month. Total eclipse of the Sun occurs February 4-5. That, along with the quintuple conjunction of planets is going to act as a disturbing, upsetting influence to a lot of good folks. Hence, the need for poise.

Watch your mental and emotional poise carefully between now and February. This is important. Make it a habit to keep calm and poised emotionally. Avoid impulsive action. Reason for this is, February's vibrations may cause you to feel "extra-confident", "extra lucky". Big danger is in trying to push your luck too far.

So go easy during February. Don't press your luck, avoid over-excitability and ... keep poised.

(5) Think Big. Create big. New Ideologies -- big new ideas and concepts for better New Age living -- are sure to be eagerly accepted by millions or more persons in the weeks and months ahead. The time between now and February can be well "invested" by you if you make a promise to yourself to "Think Big" and "Create Big".

- 33 -

All of us, whether we fully realize it or not, are now being hurtled at terrific speed into the New Age. We are being impelled to get a different viewpoint on everything... our whole frame of reference is changing...and so are WE.

We are changing because our "cosmic environment" is changing, evolving, and no living soul can escape the dynamic new influences. Each of us can, however, consciously attune ourselves to those influences...and move with the Cosmic Tide.

This Great Conjunction of February 4-5, 1962, may well be the most significant configuration of planets in your entire lifetime. Potent new rays of planetary, solar, and Super-Solar Force will be directed upon the Earth and humanity..and this fact will mark a great Turning Point for all of us.

I predict, my friend, that the "forces of darkness" that have held the center of the stage for so long, and which have worked overtime to suffocate the "spiritual man" out of his rightful position on earth...will "lose a round" in February!

I see a new Ideal about to be born in the minds of men. It will spur human evolution onward, upward, Goodward, towards more perfect and divine attainment and expression! It will act as a new Cosmic Impulse which is fully capable of affecting the whole human race on the subjective or soul level.

Under the awesome influence of The Great Conjunction of seven planets in the sign of Aquarius, a goodly amount of the vibrations" of Aquarius will, like rain, be poured upon the heads of the just and unjust alike. But it will affect the two groups differently. Persons now actively working "in the light" of true New Age understanding will be greatly strengthened by this inpouring of superphysical energies. Hence, the month of February is likely to be an exceptionally empowering and creative time for you and all New Age individuals.

This new cosmic impulse of higher energies cannot, however, make evil men good overnight. They will be confused by it and disturbed. But it is for their own good and the good of all mankind. Many will wake up and begin searching for truth about themselves and so a new "spiritual ascent" will begin. Awakened souls -- the prepared ones -- will learn of the reality and powers of the Holy Grail, which is the finding of God in man. The Urn or Chalice of Aquarius, you know, has always been associated with the idea of the Holy Grail.

It's been wonderful visiting with you again! We have shared much together, yet it is only the beginning of adventures to come. Till then, God bless and keep you!

ooo0000000

ARCHIVAL NEWSPAPER ARTICLES ON MICHAEL X

Man From Venus To Lecture Here
<u>**Santa Cruz Sentinel**</u> **(Santa Cruz, California)**
05 Nov 1959, Thu.Page 7

Man From Venus To Lecture Here

What are the people like who inhabit Venus?

Michael "X" Barton of Santa Barbara will answer these and other like questions when he lectures to members of Santa Cruz Understanding Unit 9 at 8 p.m. Saturday in the Colonial room of the St. George hotel.

The public is invited.

Barton's talk will be entitled: "The Great Venusian eMssage." He claims to have been in contact with the planet, and is author of the book "Venusian's Secret Science".

Space Craft Convention Set Here July 2,3,4
<u>**Weekly Times-Advocate**</u> **(Escondido, California)**
10 Jun 1960, Fri. Page 4

Spacecraft Convention Set Here July 2, 3, 4

The 1960 Spacecraft Convention will be July 2, 3 and 4 at Harmony Grove Camp, Escondido. It will be sponsored by Michael V. Barton (Michael X), of Los Angeles.

The program will begin at 10:30 a.m. each day. It will end at 10 p.m. July 2 and 3 and 9:30 p.m. July 4.

Tourist have their choice of 2,300 state parks in the US.

Space-Age Talk Slated Tonight
Daily Independent Journal (San Rafael, California)
17 May 1961, Wed. Page 17

Space-Age Talk
Slated Tonight

Michael X. Barton, space-age author and lecturer, will speak on "World UFO Predictions and You," this evening at 8 p.m. at Deer Park School in Fairfax.

The talk, sponsored by Understanding, Inc. Unit 31 of Marin County, deals with "the subtle techniques by which America and its people are being confused and misled today," Barton said.

Unidentified flying objects will be the feature of the talk.

Little River-- On The Coast
<u>Ukiah Daily Journal</u> (Ukiah, California)
24 May 1961, Wed. Page 12

•

Little River -- On the Coast

By HAZEL PETERSON

LITTLE RIVER -- Mr. and Mrs. Albert Haarby have as house guests their nephew, Bob Waite, of Mineral Springs, with his wife and son Freddy, a ten month old redhead. Mr. Waite, who is a Specialist 4-cl in the Army, will be leaving for Europe the first of July. Mrs. Waite plans to live in Laytonville, with an aunt, while her husband is overseas.

Sunday guests May 14 at the Hyrum Taylor home in Albion were their son Douglas Taylor of Oakland, and Mr. and Mrs. John Shakespeare and their children, Dennis, Mark, and Carla of Hayward. Mr. Shakespeare is a business associate of the younger Mr. Taylor.

Mrs. Florence Willis of Albion and Mrs. Daniel Vaughn had a very pleasant two day trip last week. They left here by bus on Wednesday, met two friends. Mrs. Catherine Shevich and Mrs. Ed Partin for lunch, after which they saw "The World of Suzy Wong," then went on to Montgomery Village to have dinner at the Saddle and Sirloin, then attended a lecture by Michael X. Barton in San Francisco, and were ready to call it a day. They returned to Santa Rosa to spend the night at the Ed Partin home. After a short visiting hour over breakfast Mrs. Partin drove the Mesdames Willis and Vaughn home.

went to Santa Rosa, on business, from there they went to San Francisco to see Mrs. Kitchen's sisters, Mrs. Harold Howell and Miss Abbie Wolter. From there they drove east to Walnut Creek, and returned home the following day with Mr. Gibbens, who recently lost his wife.

Mr. Glenn Mitchell, of Sausalito, was a house guest at the Frances Langton home last week. Mr. Mitchell is a professional photographer, and here found plenty of interesting and worthwhile subjects for his lens.

For Barbecuing
QUICKETTS

10 Pound Bag ....

Venice Ministers To Give Talks At UFO Conclave
Evening Vanguard (Venice, California)
14 May 1962, Mon. Page 2

•

Venice Ministers To Give Talks At UFO Conclave

Two ministers from Venice will address the Unidentified Flying Object Space and Science Convention scheduled June 1 and 2 at the Embassy Building at 847 S. Grand St., Los Angeles.

The men are Rev. Michael "X" Barton, and Rev. Frank E. Stranges. Rev. Stranges, who is president of the International Evangelism Crusades Inc., sponsors of the convention, will be master of ceremonies.

Slides and motion pictures of UFO will be shown at the convention which begins at 7:30 p.m. Friday and will last from 10 a.m. to 10 p.m. Saturday.

Flying Saucer Sighters
Times-Advocate (Escondido, California)
02 Jul 1962, Mon. Page 2

Earthlings Warned At Harmony Grove Meeting To Mend Ways Or Face Doom

By KEN MONDSHINE

We earthlings were warned this week end — "Mend your ways or else!" — in various ways at a meeting on the outskirts of Escondido in Harmony Grove.

For two days, more than 300 persons assembled in the shady retreat to give and compare opinions of 'mystical and metaphysical' advice uttered to them by 'wisdom from outer space'.

★ ★ ★ ★   ★ ★ ★

'Celestial' Messengers

SPEAKERS AT the two-day meeting of the Understanding, Inc., included (left to right) the Reverend George King, leader of the 'Aetherius Society, a world-wide group; R. A. (Bob) Crighton of Vista and president of the local unit of Understanding, Inc., and Michael X. Barton.

★ ★ ★ ★   ★ ★ ★

-47-

At the 'New Age Understand-orama', delegates from thruout Southern California and Arizona in orderly and quiet fashion heard and gave revelations of various mystical sects ready to warn mankind. From the advice given to many by flying saucer-men to new interpretations of the Gospel, the space around Harmony Grove was filled with the sayings of mystical and celestial sources.

The conclave, organized and conducted by R. A. (Bob) Crighton, a retired Vistan and president of the local unit of Understanding, Inc., presented all sorts of speakers from Kelvin Rowe. "My Contacts With People From Other Planets" to Michael X. Barton who disclosed some facts about flying saucers.

Tells of Revelations

Barton, under the shade of one of the many sycamore trees, revealed some of his revelations to the T-A on the last day of the meeting. He explained about his many flying saucer sightings and his last vision in April, 1962, of two beautiful 'shining blue' objects over Los Angeles.

With disappointment, he explained that he hasn't seen actual occupants, but has heard warnings, telepathically, about the reckless ways of man and his ultimate salvation.

Another 'Star' Speaker

Sitting next to him was another 'star' speaker at the meet, Riley Crabb of Vista, director of Borderland Science Research Associates, a group of 550 persons thruout the country who take an active interest (or part) in the unusual happenings along the borderland between the visible and invisible worlds.

Crabb, who also had contacted flying saucers, had his own opinions. "They're from the Moon," he quickly disclosed. "They could be from a colony of another planet settled on the lunarscope or from a highly developed Moon race."

No Royal Delegates

When asked where he received his information, the tall speaker explained that he got his knowledge from various scientific journals which expound the theory.

While the meeting wasn't honored with the presence of royal delegates from outer space as at a similar Harmony Grove meeting in 1959, space beings were vividly described by the Reverend George King, a leader of a world-wide group called the 'Aetherius Society' and the telepathic appointee for the 'Interplanetary Parliament.' The distinguished - looking Englishman explained the difference between Martians and Venusians who he said had contacted him to warn him about the approaching doom of man if he doesn't reform.

"The Martians look a lot like Earthmen, except they're shorter and of cinnamon color," he seriously explained. "They're different from the blue eyed — no pupils — Venusians. But they all have the same warning that man shouldn't go out into space since he won't be allowed to land and that he shouldn't experiment any further with nuclear weapons."

The former yoga practitioner, who received his first contact in his London apartment, left England in 1959 to come to America on the advice of 'space intelligences' to start a 'world mission.'

Old Friend

After interviewing King, this reporter ran into an old friend who was at the 1959 meeting, Dana Howard, writer and mystic, who had new revelations, molded to the signs of the time as those of many others at the two-day conclave.

She revealed how she received word from her 'way out' friends concerning the present US space program and the fate of the future astronauts who will fly into the heavens. But our talk came down to earth when Dana interrupted our conversation to speak to one of her followers and to pack up her booklets for the return to her Palm Springs home.

Others also were packing, some were leaving for Mount Shasta to another meeting to see others honored with 'out-of-space' contacts; while others were preparing to leave for their homes to wait for further signs from the sky.

You are cordially invited to a most interesting
'New Age' lecture
The Los Angeles Times **(Los Angeles, California)**
27 Sep 1962, Thu. Page 36

to be ruled by men in high places that betrayed their own sex with the false idea of woman suffrage.

"The spirit of the American idea died with that infamous betrayal of the home and relationship between husband and wife.

"Woman should never have gotten the vote. Why did we give in to them?" (Signed) A. C. Lundberg, Huntington Park.

—It was the bloomers, A. C. They were enough to turn any man's head.

★

"You are cordially invited to a most interesting 'New Age' lecture to be given Sept. 28 by Michael X. Barton.

"At this talk, vital knowledge regarding your Conscious Continuation on to the next plane will be revealed to you by Michael. He will tell you of his own real experiences on the 'astral plane,' and give you the full benefit of his observations and conclusions.

"You will benefit in six ways by attending this lecture:

"You will discover how the Body of Light is built. You will learn about the Lower Astral Plane. You will learn about the Higher Astral Plane. You will be given four methods by which you may accomplish Astral Projection safely. You will hear the true story of what was found on the moon by one who went there in his astral body. You will find out how 'familiars' are created, and how to protect yourself from psychic 'black magic.'

"If you have not as yet attended one of our meetings, now is the time to come. You will have the pleasure of seeing many of your friends here." (Signed) Aquarian Cosmic Color Fellowship, L.A.

—I wondered where they all went.

'New Age Truth Rally' Set Saturday, Sunday At Harmony Grove

Times-Advocate (Escondido, California)

21 Nov 1962, Wed. Page 11

'New-Age Truth Rally' Set Saturday, Sunday At Harmony Grove

Escondido area residents will have a chance Saturday and Sunday to learn about Martians, Venusians, flying saucers a n d other extraterrestrial matters at the "New-Age Truth Rally" in Harmony Grove. Michael X. Barton will be master of ceremonies.

Discussions at the meeting will center around such topics as "The Coming World Peril," "The Seven Rays of Healing," and other challenges concerned with the mind, health and space phenomena.

Hamid Bey, master of coptic wisdom, will speak on "The Power of the Mind" and "Temple Training" at 1:30 p.m. Saturday, Barton said. He said this is Bey's first guest appearance at Harmony Grove.

The two-day rally begins at 9:15 a.m. Saturday and concludes at 4:45 p.m. Sunday.

•Speakers Announced For New Age Convocation

<u>Times-Advocate</u> (Escondido, California)

04 Jan 1963, Fri. Page 9

Speakers Announced For New Age Convocation Here

Speakers have been announced for the New Age Convocation to be held Saturday and Sunday at Harmony Grove.

Michael X. Barton of Los Angeles will be the chief speaker. The title of his Saturday evening talk is "Forever Young, Forever Immortal." Sunday afternoon, he will discuss extrasensory perception and give a demonstration of psychic precognition of coming events.

During the session Saturday morning, Violet Ballard Barton will speak about Mark Twain as a mystic helper of mankind. "How to Contact Celestial Vibrations" is the topic for Dr. Nephi Cottam Saturday afternoon.

Sunday morning activities will be highlighted by a ceremonial christening of Harmony Grove as, what the New Age group calls, "a dedicated center of higher spiritual teachings and New Age light."

A panel discussion Sunday afternoon will explore the mysterious events surrounding the recent death of Unidentified Flying Objects researcher Gloria Lee, author of the book "Why We Are Here."

New Aid Truth Rally
Times-Advocate (Escondido, California)
20 Apr 1963, Sat. Page 4

✦ **HARMONY GROVE**
Spiritualist Association — 745 7147
Sat., Sun., New Aid Truth Rally —
Michael X. Barton
✦ **HOUSE OF PRAYER**

New Age Lecturer

The San Bernardino County Sun (San Bernardino, California)

03 Apr 1964, Fri. Page 12

•

n

New-Age Lecture

Riverside unit of "Understanding" will present Michael X. Barton in a New-Age lecture at 2:45 p.m. Sunday at the Izaak Walton Hall, Dexter Drive, Fairmount Park, Riverside.

n
b
e
o
r

Saucers Still Fly

Redlands Daily Facts (Redlands, California)

04 Apr 1964, Sat. Page 5

Saucers Still Fly

Michael X. Barton will relate his latest flying saucer experiences tomorrow at 2:45 p.m. at Isaac Walton Hall, Dexter Drive, Fairmont Park, Riverside, at a meeting of "Understanding".

Flying Saucer Lecturer Slated

<u>Southwest Topics-Wave</u> (Los Angeles, California)

21 Feb 1965, Sun. Page 13

Flying saucer lecturer slated

Michael X. Barton, lecturer, writer, and researcher in the field of flying saucers will address members of the Inglewood Unit of Understanding Saturday, 8 p.m., in the clubhouse at 820 Java street.

Barton's topic will be "UFOs, the Fifth Dimension, and You," announced C. R. Gahlbeck, president.

UFO'S AND THE INCREDIBLE SEARCH
The Los Angeles Times (Los Angeles, California)
17 Oct 1965, Sun. Page 633

•

"U.F.O.'S AND THE INCREDIBLE SEARCH"
by Michael X. Barton, sponsored by Inglewood Unit of Understanding; Business and
Professional Women's Clubhouse, 820 Java
St., Inglewood, 8 p.m.

York's Carnegie
tour of Europe
dour she's back

Los Angeles Times CALENDAR, SUNDAY, OCTOBER 17, 1965

UFO Talk Slated
<u>The Los Angeles Times</u> (Los Angeles, California)
05 Nov 1965, Fri. Page 3.

UFO Talk Slated

SANTA ANA — "UFOs and the Incredible Search for Dr. Halsey" will be the subject of an illustrated talk by Michael X. Barton at a meeting of Orange County Unit No. 7 of Understanding tonight at 8 in the Community Center Clubhouse, 1104 W. 8th St.

Philosopher To Speak
Redlands Daily Facts (Redlands, California)
07 Dec 1965, Tue. Page 5

Philosopher To Speak

Michael X. Barton, billed as a writer and lecturer on the "New Age" philosophy, will speak at a gathering slated for 8 p.m. Thursday in the Cottage of Yucaipa Park, 12444 Seventh street. "The Incredible Search" is scheduled to be the topic of the address, sponsored by Understanding, incorporated, unit 61.

Man in Space Symposium to Get Underway Here Tomorrow

The Dunsmuir News (Dunsmuir, California)

02 Jun 1966, Thu. Page 1

•

Man In Space Symposium To Get Underway Here Tomorrow

"Man In Space", a Symposium to be held June 3, 4, 5 in Dunsmuir, is scheduled to bring enthusiasts from all over the State to hear lectures and discussions on the much publicised phenomena known as UFO's.

According to coordinator for the meetings, Charles Thomas of Mount Shasta, reservations for the unusual get-to-gether are coming in rapidly the past few days. Thomas thinks that before the three day affair is over as many as two thousand people will have visited the Symposium under the direction of Dr. Daniel Fry of Merlin, Oregon and his organization called, Understanding, Inc.

Thomas said that Dr. Fry is to introduce the principal speakers for the meetings at the opening sessions during a Smorgasbard Luncheon at the House of Glass Friday evening at 6:00 o'clock. There is to be a Social Hour from 5:00 to 6:00 preceeding the dinner hour.

There are free movies to be showwn during the evening Friday ahead of the dinner speakers with the most popular one "The Day The Earth Stood Still", a commentary being given by Dr. Fry.

All showings will be at the Elementary auditorium, down-town Dunsmuir.

Some of the speakers during the sessions, said Thomas will be Dr. Frank B. Salisbury, of the department of Botany and Pathology at the U. of Colorado, spaking on "Aspects of Life on Mars."

Colonel Harry May of the U. S. active Airforce Reserve, to be speaking on flying objects from an official standpoint. Hs is a pilot and has been reported to have seen a number of UFO's.

Mr. Michael X. Barton, Ufologist of California, will tell of his experiences while hunting a downed plane in the Sierras in recent years.

Hope Troxell, Independence, California, will speak on "Evolved Man of the Stars", Miss Troxell is from the School of Thou-

Hope Troxell, Independence, California, will speak on "Evolved Man of the Stars", Miss Troxell is from the School of Thought, of Independence.

Gayne Meyers of Auburn, will tell the "Story of Dolloran". Sidney Patrick of Watsonville, will tell of his experiences near Monterey, California last year, when he was taken aboardd a space vehicle, and talked with the people aboard.

The formal opening will be at 10 a.m. Saturday morning, June 4th, at the Dunsmuir Elementary School, Florence Ave. in Downtown Dunsmuir.

Thomas says that a new song, "Mt. Shasta Calls" will be sung by Miss Miriam Amburn, will be featured at opening formalkies, with the color guard presented by the Explorer Scout Troop of Dunsmuir.

It has also been announced that on both Saturday and Sunday, the Chamber of Commerce of Mt. Shasta will conduct tours to the mountain by bus. There is to be no charge for the ride.

For further information as to the various subjects to be discussed you may phone travelers Hotel in Dunsmuir.

Author to Speak on UFOOs and Prophecy
<u>The San Bernardino County Sun</u>

(San Bernardino, California)

23 Sep 1966, Fri. Page 42

•

Author to Speak on UFOs and Prophecy

Author and lecturer Michael X. Barton will speak to San Bernardino Unit 71 of Understanding, Inc. in a public lecture at 2:30 p.m. Sunday.

The lecture, "UFOs and World Prophecy," will be at the American Legion Hall, 732 N. Sierra Way, San Bernardino.

Church News In Brief
The Modesto Bee (Modesto, California)
04 Nov 1966, Fri. Page 16

Church News In Brief

Approximately 150 persons are expected to attend the annual Foreign Students Dinner at 6:30 p.m. next Friday in the Maze Boulevard Christian Church Fellowship Hall, 725 Maze Blvd., Modesto.

International students attending the Modesto Junior College will be guests at the dinner and the program following.

The House of the Lord Mission has moved from its 9th Street location to 902 E. Hatch Road. The Rev. R. D. Sinner said the new quarters include a chapel, a kitchen and a house for mission staff. Services are held at 7:30 o'clock each night.

Prayer life will be emphasized at the Modesto Seventh-day Adventist Church, 17th and H Streets, beginning at 11 a.m. tomorrow. A special week will include nightly prayer services at 7:30 o'clock in the church.

The Universal Life Church, 1776 Poland Road, Modesto, will hold a convention tonight, tomorrow and Sunday. Tonight's service will begin at 7 o'clock.

Speakers including Michael X. Barton of Los Angeles will consider spacecraft, spiritualism, life after death, life on other planets and hypnosis and healing.

The Northern California Conference, United Church of Christ, will convene from 10 a.m. to 3:30 p.m. tomorrow in Oakland. Modesto delegates are expected to attend.

William Hunt, state park naturalist from Donner State Park, will speak on "The Donner Story" at 7 p.m. Wednesday in the Modesto Corps, The Salvation Army. The public is invited.

Motion pictures from Jerusalem will be shown at 7 o'clock tonight and tomorrow night in the General Baptist Church, Dover Drive and Midway Tract Road.